Life Is Now!

Simple Slow Days Are The Best

Cindy Thurmond

Cindy's Choice Books
An Imprint of Overview Publishing
USA

This edition published by:
Cindy's Choice Books
An imprint of Overview Publishing
P.O. Box 16763
Atlanta, Georgia 30321

Copyright © 2006, Cindy Thurmond

ISBN 0-9760685-1-6

All rights reserved. No part of this book may be used or reproduced in any matter whatsoever without the written permission of the publisher except in the case of reprints in the context of reviews.

Printed and bound in China.

Thurmond, Cindy, 1961-
   Life Is Now : a guide to enjoying and remembering the simple things in life.
   ISBN: 0976068516

First Edition March 2006

To My Wonderful Husband, Patrick

Thank you for allowing me endless hours on the computer without question.

To: _____

From: _____

For the best in all of us waiting to reach the surface.

A Message From The Author

I am proud to make this book available to all who need it and that's probably everyone!

This book was designed to help you to remember that life is truly now. Saver every moment and be a child at heart.

Do you remember the exciting silly fun things you did as a child, Why not still do them? Or more?

Point to Ponder;

If life is truly now-why do so many people forget and spend so much time thinking about what could happen and possibly never will?

Life Is Now

Enjoy.

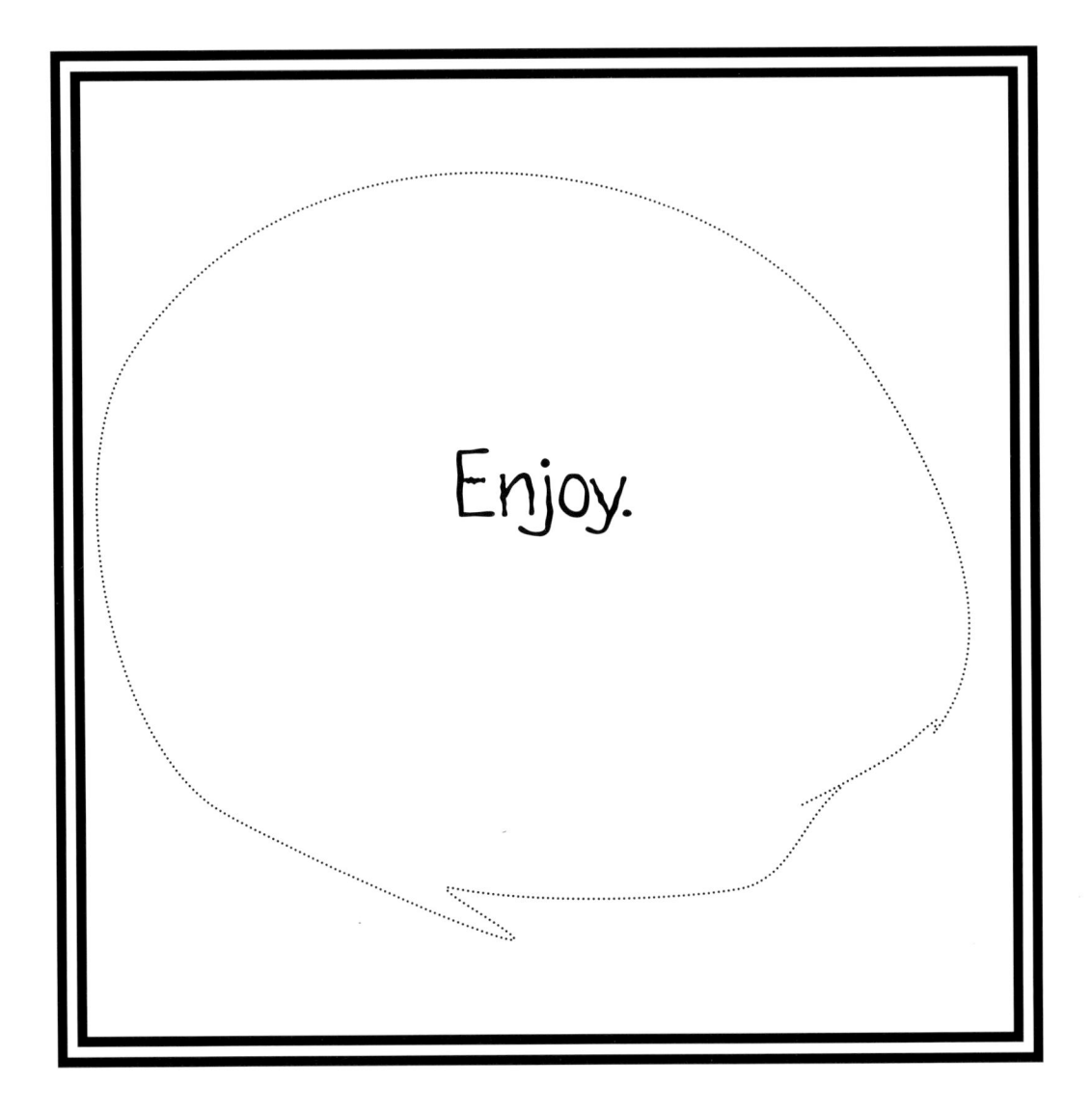

Drink lemonade.

Eat pizza for breakfast.

Watch a scary movie by yourself.

Roll in the leaves.

Sip
on cheap wine
as you swing
on the
back porch
swing.

Run through the sprinklers.

Pick

a

dandelion

&

blow it

into the wind.

Eat Candy.

Throw a Party.

Climb

a

tree.

Stay humble.

Pick

your

own

berries.

Pretend you are invisible.

Sing.
Even if you
think you
can not.

Go on a bus ride to nowhere in particular.

Find the big dipper in the night sky.

Climb a mountain-- even a small one.

Watch the planes fly overhead.

Slurp spaghetti noodle by noodle.

Appreciate your successes.

Stay

up

all night---

one

night.

Eat

slices

of

cheese----

slice by slice.

Go Barefoot.

Do something you've always wanted to do.

Wear colorful undies.

Cry
at the
movies.

Don't keep up with the neighbors.

Ride

a

rollercoaster.

Watch fish swim in a river.

Be silly.

Dance with all your heart & soul.

Dream daily.

Ride a bicycle to the store.

Be
Curious.

Follow

a

butterfly.

Save all your old love notes.

Wear purple.

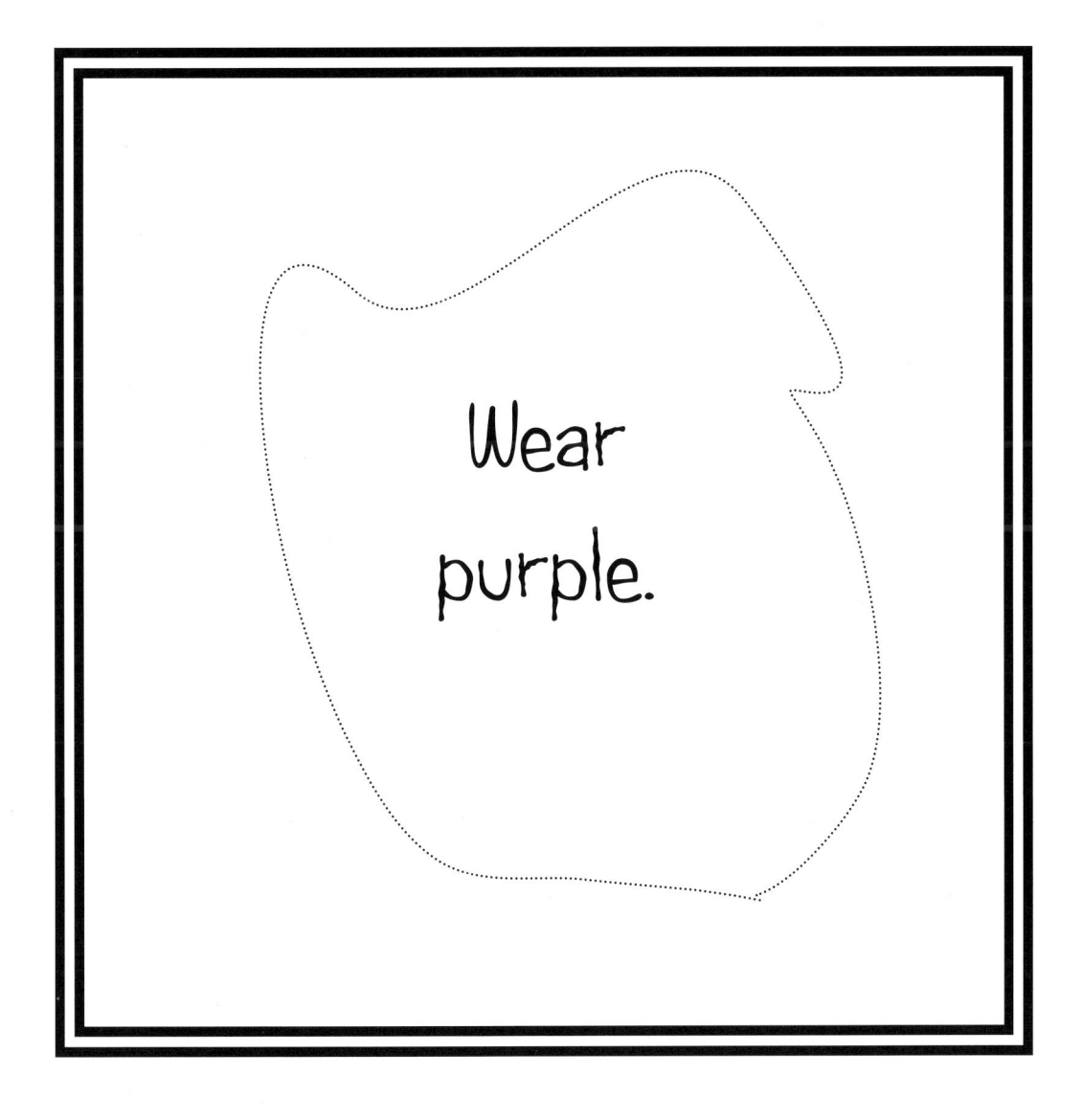

Build a fire

&

roast

marshmallows.

Watch the clouds changing shapes.

Swing
at a play ground
in the
morning sun.

Wear cheap jewelry.

Read
a good book
by flashlight
under the

covers.

Watch cartoons.

Watch

a candle

flicker

in the dark.

Go see the ocean.

Enjoy someone's company.

Fly
a
kite.

Camp out in your backyard.

Hide the mirror for a day.

Plant

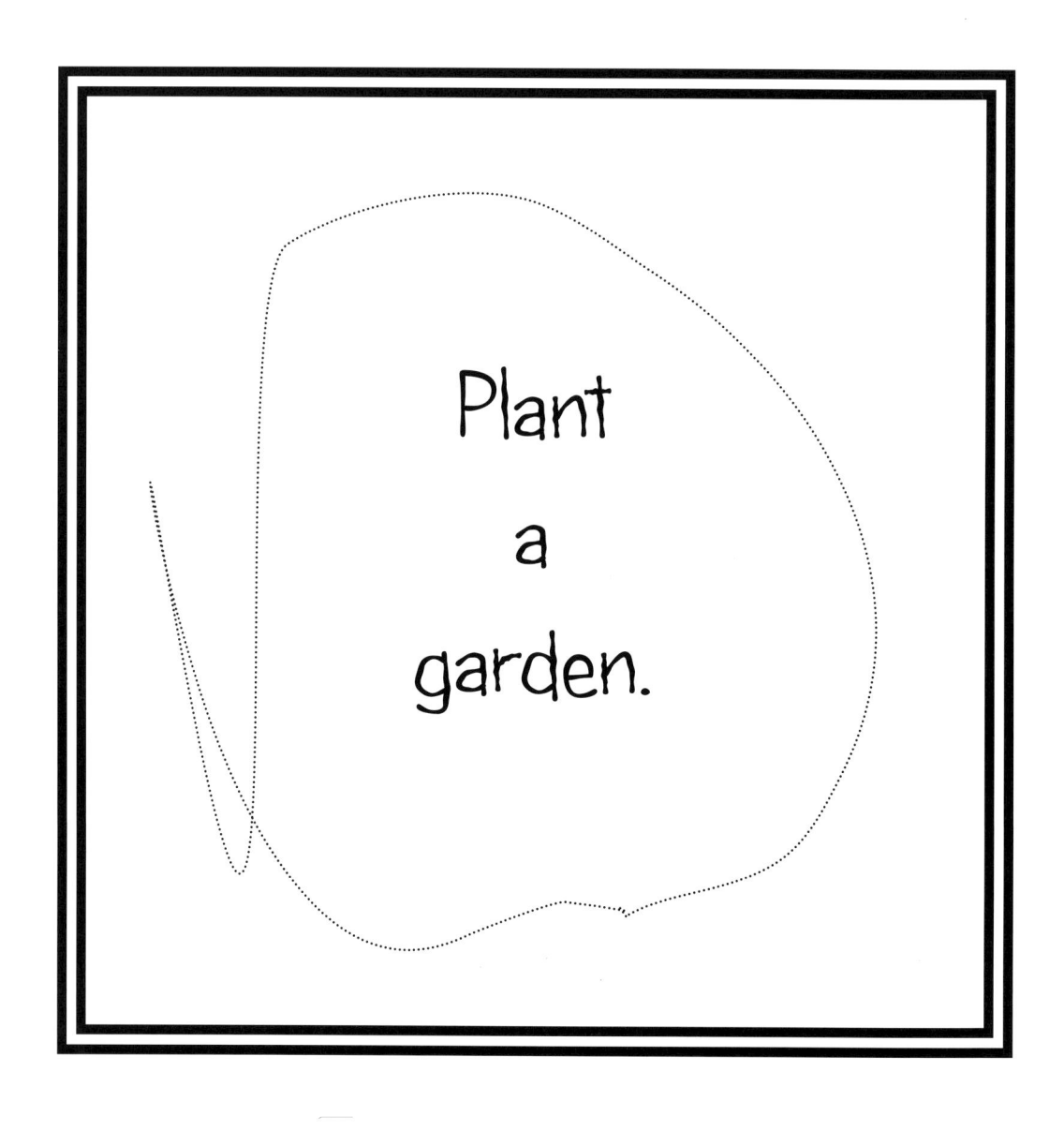

a

garden.

Follow your passions.

Get your

hair cut

in an unique style---

so

unlike you!

Wear a goofy hat.

Pick flowers by the roadside.

Don't work late today.

Help
a child
or
elderly person.

Watch

a balloon

float

away.

Give

away

one

favorite thing.

Eat an ice cream cone.

Wear dark sunglasses.

Splash in puddles.

Send a card to a friend for no reason.

Eat popcorn in the bed.

Go to the Zoo.

Kiss

a special someone

on the cheek

today.

Say thank you--
often.

Play
hide & seek
with a child
or
your mate.

Smile at yourself.

Catch tadpoles in a jar.

Take
a long
walk.

Cook

a

gourmet meal

for yourself only--

eat by candlelight.

Watch the lightning in the summer evening sky.

Laugh at a not so funny joke.

Write down your thoughts.

Clean the house today or better yet not.

Walk in the rain without an umbrella.

Take a

bubble bath

or a

long hot shower.

Give all your pennies to charity.

Surprise someone with something special.

Wear pajamas all weekend.

Find

a

mentor.

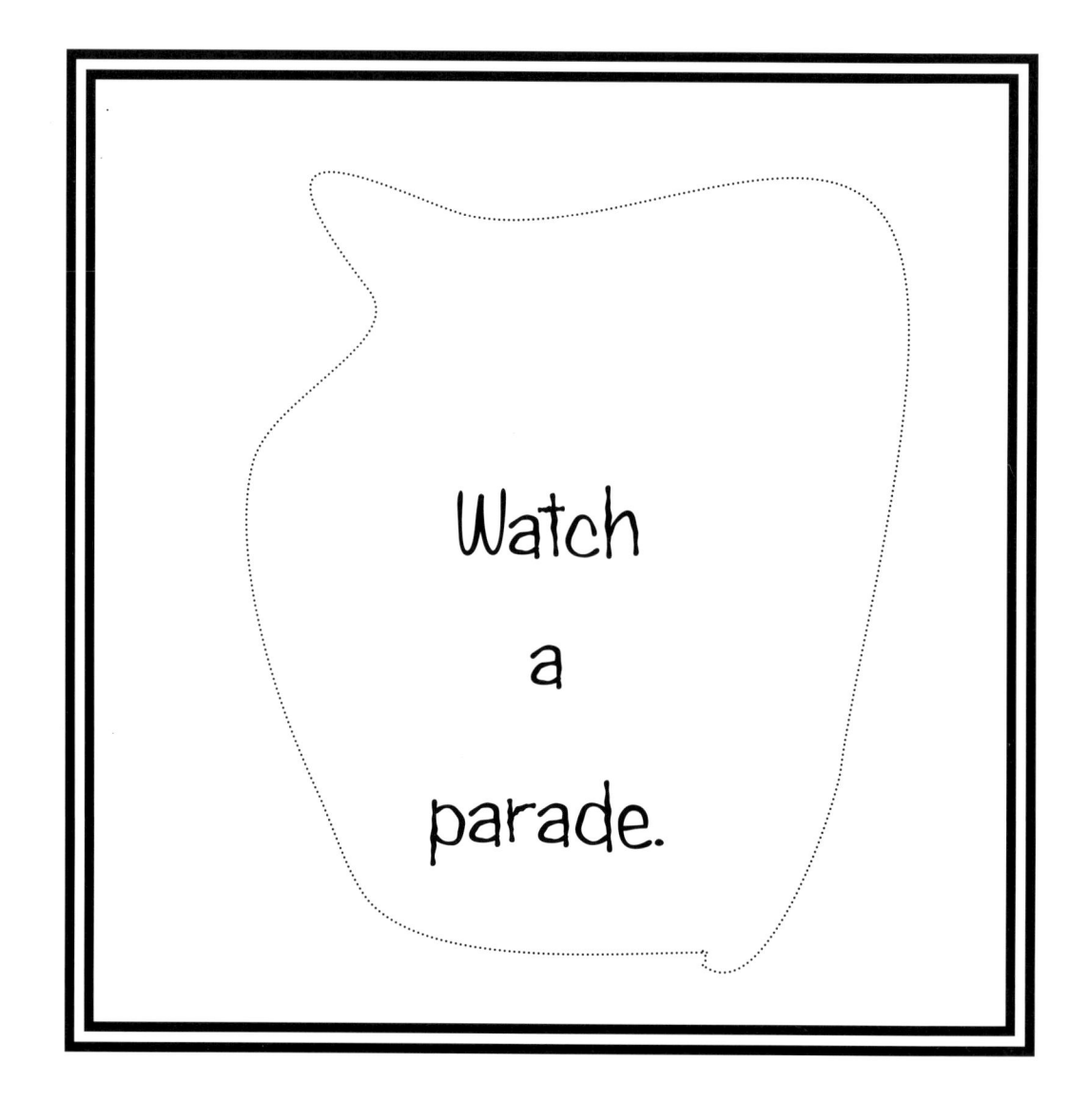

Watch

a

parade.

Experience romance.

Lay
in the
grass.

Go
skinny dipping
just once
in your life.

Go

on a

picnic.

Go ahead----
Eat
the
whole bag
of
potato chips
without feeling guilty.

Catch fireflies in the night.

Call Home.

Live

for

today.

Wear short shorts.

Skip

over

the

cracks

in the

sidewalk.

Watch a sunrise or sunset.

Pick apples from your neighbors tree.

Blow soap bubbles into the wind.

Just one more thought for you. Remember Life Is Now!

Once

again

Enjoy!

Other Books by Cindy Thurmond

What If There Were No Colors?
ISBN: 0-9760685-0-8

Cindy's son, Nicholas, always told her
   ---- Life is Now ----- mom.
So I guess life is now.

Cindy Thurmond was born in LaGrange, Georgia.
She has three adult children,
         Christina, Nicholas, & Michael.
She currently resides in McDonough, Georgia
   with her husband, Patrick,
       and two cats, Kacey, and Snowflake.
   Of course, her favorite pal, her dog (not Pat's) PeeDee
   lives with her too.